My name is:

_____

Dedication

Special thanks are extended:

To the Lammers Family for being so special

Midnight Mass

Midnight Mass on Christmas—Simply Extraordinary

This is the story of an eight-year-old boy who finally gets to serve as an acolyte at Midnight Mass on Christmas (Eve). He then religiously serves every year until he graduates after an illness almost takes him out of the picture.

This story is true. The big event took a lot of preparations. In fact, it began the day before as all the servers got to take their red cassocks and surplices home, so the moms could all fine tune them for the next day's big event. It was the moms' job to make sure all was perfect for the grand procession.

The story brings in the dad of the family whose pre-Christmas mail route always took him into some happy and festive neighborhoods. The people were just as happy as the dad for some early Christmas celebrating. The neighbors showed their appreciation in many ways including enjoying a tad of beverage with their trusty postman and of course they gave lots of gifts including cash. Dad's coming home was always a big deal as he displayed the fruits of his festive day to all the children.

The hard work of all the preparations would pay off in a glorious tribute to Christ the Lord and the heavenly hosts. You will enjoy reading about how this miracle on Christmas unfolded after the grand celebration of The Solemn High Mass at St. Francis. You won't want to put this book down. It will give you a non-removable Christmas smile.

JOHN P. LAMMERS

Referenced Material: *Standard Disclaimer:* The information in this book has *been obtained through personal and third party observations, interviews, and copious research. Where unique information has been provided or extracted from other sources, those sources are acknowledged within the text of the book itself or at the end of the chapter in the Sources Section. Thus, there are no formal footnotes nor is there a bibliography section. Any picture that does not have a source was taken from various sites on the Internet with no credit attached. If resource owners would like credit in the next printing, please email publisher.*

Published by: LETS GO PUBLISH!
Publisher   Brian P. Kelly
Email: info@letsgopublish.com
Web site   www.letsgopublish.com

Library of Congress Copyright Information Pending
Book Cover Design by Brian W. Kelly
Editor—Brian P. Kelly

ISBN Information: The International Standard Book Number (ISBN) is a unique machine-readable identification number, which marks any book unmistakably. The ISBN is the clear standard in the book industry. 159 countries and territories are officially ISBN members. The Official ISBN For this book is on the outside cover:
ISBN 978-1-947402-21-8

The price for this work is: **$7.95 USD**

10	9	8	7	6	5	4	3	2	1

Release Date: November 2017

Publisher's Note: *Please check out www.letsgopublish.com for BK books & to read the latest version of my heartfelt acknowledgments updated for this book. Click the bottom item of the Main menu!*

Merry Christmas

Table of Contents

Chapter 1 A New Altar Boy

JOHN P. LAMMERS
TEANECK, NJ-C 1947

Pure Anticipation

I have been going to Midnight Mass on Christmas since I was eight years old and a brand-new altar boy at St. Francis in Ridgefield Park, NJ. It has always been something extraordinary and, at that time, my father was always a special part of it.

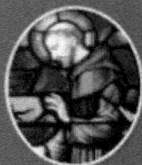

ST. FRANCIS OF ASSISI PARISH
RIDGEFIELD PARK, NEW JERSEY

Midnight Mass on Christmas was a very significant event in the lives of Catholics who lived in the first half of the twentieth century; especially so if you were an altar boy and the son of John Henry Lammers. The nuns at St. Francis and my father always made sure it was special. The anticipation was always so great that I am incredulous that the actual event was as meaningful and exciting as the time leading up to it.

Preparations were important

Of course preparations always began days in advance of Christmas when Father Butscher brought all of the altar boys to the church for practice. Father and the sisters made sure that all would be perfect for the celebration of the birth of Christ.

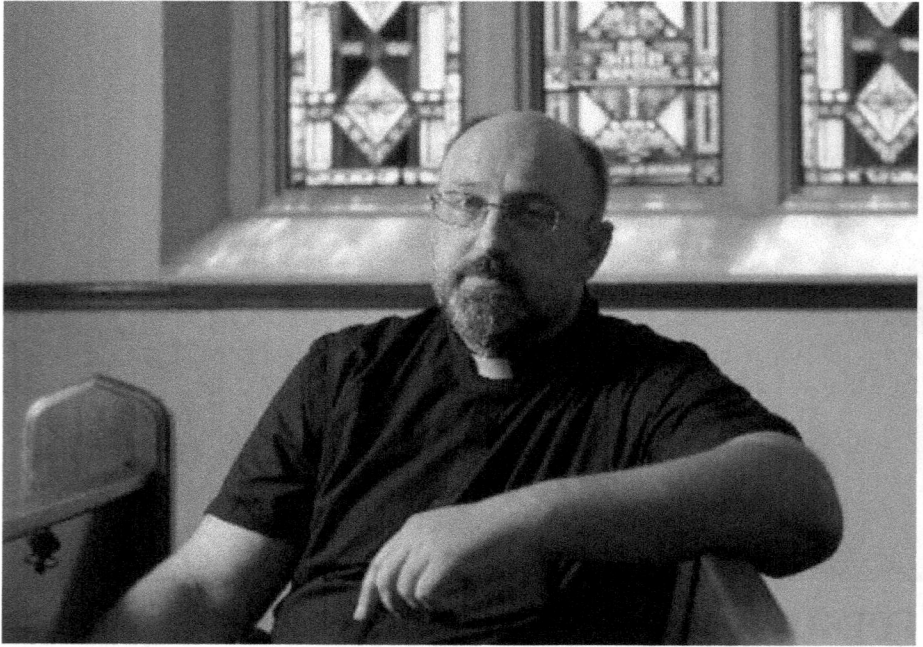

The church would be packed and no eight year old boy was about to embarrass Sister Catherine Josephine and her Sisters or Father. It was then that we found out what position each of us would take for the grand celebration.

There were the cross bearers, candle bearers, torch bearers, acolytes and grunts. The first-time altar boys were the grunts and filled out the procession. It was also at that time that the red cassocks came out of storage and Sister Raymond made sure that every boy had one that fit.

Making sure we looked perfect

She also gave each of us a white surplice and white collar with rounded points that we wore with a large red bow tie. The entire outfit was to be taken home so my mother could wash, starch and press them. Mine were always the best.

Chapter 2 The Full Event

The tree was up when Dad got home

The event began early on the day before Christmas with the anticipation of the Mass and also with the anxiety of waiting for Dad to come home from work. By then the tree was up and decorated and ready for the arrival of Santa Claus.

Dad was carrying his mail route twice a day at that time and that made for a long day especially on Christmas Eve when the social stops were many. By the time he got home he was tired and a little smoky from the few drops of the creator that he had shared with the people on his route.

We couldn't wait to see Dad

My sister and brother and I were lined up as he came through the front door with a big smile on his face and the pockets of his uniform greatcoat bulging with the Christmas gifts he received from the people on his route.

Since he was the world's greatest mailman, and loveable besides, the gifts were many and very generous. He would greet us by hoisting each of us on his shoulders then put us down and unload his pockets on the floor for us to ogle and count the cash. There was always a lot and sometimes there were other gifts as well.

One of his customers worked for Kaywoodie Pipe and he had a few of those in his drawer. He didn't smoke a pipe so he gave most of them away. There were others but I don't remember what they were.

Feeling good was feeling good

The Christmas tree was in the corner of the living room and we sometimes lay under it, in the space that would later be occupied with our own gifts, when counting Dad's.

Mom, of course would give him the bad eye because he was feeling pretty good, but she made no issue of it because she knew how hard he worked.

Chapter 3 Time for Dinner & a Nap

Fish cakes a plenty

By the time he had taken his shower he was settled down a little and was then ready for his usual dinner of fish cakes and spaghetti with tomato soup for sauce. Mom: "Jackie, Go down to Pete Luhrs' deli and get some fish cakes for your father's dinner".

Pete's was only a short walk through the outfield of our sandlot ball field and I must have made that trip ten thousand times, there and to the other stores on Queen Anne Road. In those days the eve of major a Feast Day was always a day of abstinence and fish cakes were the only fish that Dad would eat. It was that or scrambled eggs.

A sleep remedy for Midnight Mass

Once supper was finished he would read the paper and then he and I would take a nap, he because he was tired and I because I didn't want to fall asleep on the altar. The time from this point on was always the most special for me because we spent it alone together.

My brother and sister went to their beds for the night and I went with Dad for the nap. That nap is among my fondest memories because it was during the time before we fell asleep that we would have some very good private conversations.

A boy and his dad—special time

Nothing was ever too deep because I was only a young boy but I most remember him teaching me to speak German and to count in German, which I can still do.

He even sang Silent Night –Stille Nacht- in German. Whatever the topic it always made me feel special because it was just him and me and I knew, even if it was only for the moment, that he had special feelings for me. As I grew older I came to the realization that it was not only for the moment.

Chapter 4 Time to Get Up for Mass

Ten P.M. and all is well!

At ten o'clock it was time for Mom to come back into the picture and wake us up to get ready to go. It always took us a while to shake off the sleep but we could not be late under any circumstances: Father Butscher was a tyrant.

Wake up sleepy heads

Mom would have cocoa made for us and after a brush of the teeth for me and a shave for Dad we would dress, retrieve the cassock, surplice, and collar and tie that Mom had gotten ready.

He would check the shine on my shoes and we would head for St. Francis. Dad would rather die than go to church in anything but his best suit and a clean shirt, so he looked pretty spiffy.

He also smelled good from the after-shave lotion he always used on special occasions. Usually he just used witch hazel but not tonight.

Chapter 5 Off to St. Francis Church

Don't mess up the wardrobe!

We left the house with the pungent smell of the fresh Christmas tree in our nostrils. As we went out the door there was the usual admonition from Mom not to wrinkle the cassock and surplice that she had cleaned, starched and ironed, no easy chore in those days before modern appliances and no-iron fabrics.

Brrrrrrhhhh!!!

The second hand Ford that was Dad's car-
it was a 1936 model- had a heater that didn't
work all that well and so there was no hope of
escaping the cold of a late December night. I
didn't care because I was alone with my Dad
and we were going to a special place for a
special event.

It really didn't matter anyway because St.
Francis was only a half mile trip down Bergen
Avenue, a trip that I would make many times

in my years at St. Francis, and we would be inside the church in only minutes.

ST. FRANCIS CHURCH, RIDGEFIELD PARK, N. J.

The small parking lot was gravel at that time and I can still hear the crunch of the tires as we pulled in through the opening in the cyclone fence that surrounded the school yard; that is if there was no snow on the ground.

It was at this time that we had to part as Dad went to the church vestibule, where he would station himself, with some of his friends, and fulfill his duties as an usher. It was not an easy job as the church would be crowded and people would have on heavy coats and take up more space than usual.

The fat ladies were always the first to get a little huffy as he asked them to move in and make room for others. He never had much trouble because he was handsome, polite and smiled a lot.

Chapter 6 Good Evening Father

The calm before the storm

I entered the church through the side door that led into the priests' sacristy and, after saying "Good evening father" to each of the priests, made my way through the hallway that went behind the altar to what was called the altar boys' sacristy. Before long it would become as active as a beehive with a stick poked in it.

There were usually two sisters, Sr. Raymond and Sr. Grace, who had charge of the altar boys, moving at speeds that were thought impossible for women in floor length habits; and without making any noise except for the swish of the habits.

As the boys came in the room swelled with bodies all squirming to get into 'uniform'. The starched collars always gave us the most difficulty and it was the rare boy who could button his collar without Sister's help.

A motley bunch ready for service

The boys were from the fourth to the eighth grades so some of the bodies were pretty big. It was like a rush hour subway car in there. Somehow the sisters made order out of chaos and, by the time we lined up for the procession through the church we looked like The First Marines in their dress uniforms.

Chapter 7 It's Time for the Procession

Everybody lined up perfectly

The procession began in the priests' sacristy and entered the nave through an inside door that opened on the side aisle of the church.

It was lead by the cross bearer and two candle bearers followed by acolytes, torch bearers and grunts with the priests at the end.

Since it was to be a Solemn High Mass there were three priests preceded by a master of ceremonies.

As the side door opened into the church and the crossbearer became visible the congregation would stand and Miss Ries, the organist, would begin the opening bars of *Adeste Fidelis*, which the boys would begin singing on cue. It was at that moment that the preparations paid off. It was magnificent.

Golden voices from heaven

Some of the boys, I was not one of them, had golden voices and the sound would have brought tears to Bing Crosby's eyes. God must have been smiling because some of those boys were rascals when away from the regimentation that the nuns imposed on us.

When we came to the end of the side aisle we processed through the vestibule in order to make our way into the center aisle from which we would enter the sanctuary for Mass.

It was then that Dad and I would meet fleetingly as he gave me his nod of recognition and approval from his usher's station. That was a special moment, both for me and for him and I could always tell by his look that he was proud of me. I am sure that I reminded him of himself at the same age as he was when an altar boy at St. Brigid's in North Bergen.

Then it was up the center isle and the singing continued until the entire procession was inside the sanctuary and the altar rail was closed.

Chapter 8 The Solemn High Traditional Mass

All altar boys had a role in the Mass

Then began the most beautiful thing this side of Heaven—the Solemn High Traditional Mass—and we boys were an integral part of it. Some of us, like the censor bearer, had an active role but most were there to add to the beauty of the ceremony and we did our jobs well.

There was no choice, of course, because we were always under the watchful eyes of the good Sisters who trained us. I am sure that there are groups who did it far better than we, as in the great cathedrals, but no one ever did it with more fervor than those twenty five boys in Ridgefield Park, NJ.

Must be seen to be appreciated

The Mass itself is indescribable and must be seen and understood for its beauty and reverence to be fully appreciated. For almost two hours the unbloody sacrifice of the cross transcends earthly things and brings focus to the birth of the One Who made the sacrifice.

The grand exit

When one is a ten-year-old boy those thoughts never come to mind but their roots are planted by the splendor of the event. Once it was complete the altar rail was reopened and the procession retraced its steps down the center aisle and up the side aisle to the sacristy as Miss Ries played and the boys sang just as they had upon entry.

Chapter 9 The Trip Home

Tired after the long day

This was my last chance to see Dad before I met him in the parking lot for the trip home. His look was the same only a little more tired. He had been awake since 5:00 the previous morning and had worked a ten-hour day.

The trip home was always a lot more quiet than was the trip to the church as I was tired also. It always seemed to be clear and cold, a Stille Nacht, as we headed back up Bergen Avenue to our house on Tessen St.

The other thing on my mind was, of course, the anticipation of the gifts now under the tree, having been placed there by Mom while we were gone.

Receiving them on Christmas Eve was a privilege accorded to me as the oldest and by virtue of the fact that by the time we got home Christmas had already arrived.

Chapter 10 A Great Experience Every Year

Bing Crosby held back his tears

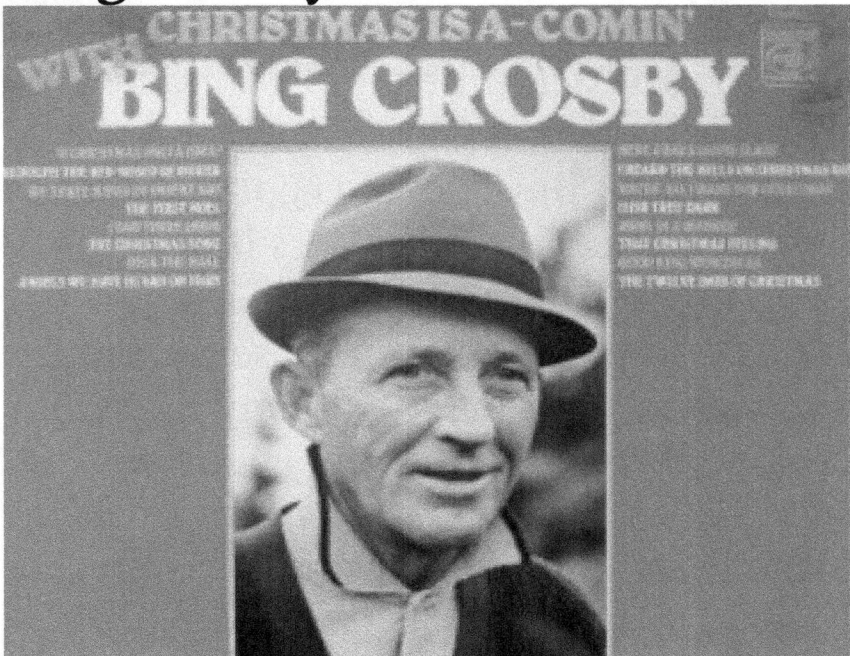

As each year of my service as an altar boy passed I moved up through the ranks and eventually made it to cross bearer but my singing voice never evolved to the point that it would make Bing Crosby cry. But the event was always the same and the special tie to my father that it brought remained strong.

Mumps and a senior altar boy

The Mass that remains most vivid in my memory was that of my eighth grade at St. Francis. It was at that time that I contracted the mumps just prior to Christmas and it looked like Father Butscher was going to have to get someone else to be the cross bearer.

We never saw a doctor in those days and my mom was the sole judge as to my fitness for any activity. She, being as tough as she was and my father being as devout as he was, it didn't take them long to make the decision that, even though I had missed school, I would not miss Midnight Mass.

Sister Raymond was surprised to see me with my swollen neck, but she was glad that I was there and squeezed me into the collar. And so my record of contiguous service at Midnight Mass remained intact and once again the special night was ours, father and son, John Henry and John Paul, and remains in my memory of him forever.

Thank you Mom and Dad for a great life!

John P. Lammers

Merry Christmas

Other books by Let's Go Publish!: (amazon.com, and Kindle)

Please take a run out to amazon.com/author/brianwkelly when you have time to find another book that you might enjoy.

The Bill of Rights By Founder James Madison Refresh *your knowledge of the specific rights granted to all*
Great Players in Army Football Great Army Football played by great players..
Great Coaches in Army Football Army's coaches are all great.
Great Moments in Army Football Army Football at its best.
Great Moments in Florida Gators Football **Gators Football from the start. This is the book.**
Great Moments in Clemson Football CU Football at its best. This is the book.
Great Moments in Florida Gators Football **Gators** Football from the start. This is the book.
The **Constitution Companion.** A Guide to Reading and Comprehending the Constitution
The Constitution by Hamilton, Jefferson, & Madison – Big type and in English
PATERNO: The Dark Days After Win # 409. Sky began to fall within days of win # 409.
JoePa 409 Victories: Say No More! Winningest Division I-A football coach ever
American College Football: The Beginning From before day one football was played.
Great Coaches in Alabama Football **Challenging the coaches of every other program!**
Great Coaches in Penn State Football **the Best Coaches in PSU's football program**
Great Players in Penn State Football **The best players in PSU's football program**
Great Players in Notre Dame Football **The best players in ND's football program**
Great Coaches in Notre Dame Football **The best coaches in any football program**
Great Players in Alabama Football from Quarterbacks to offensive Linemen Greats!
Great Moments in Alabama Football AU Football from the start. This is the book.
Great Moments in Penn State Football PSU Football, start--games, coaches, players,
Great Moments in Notre Dame Football ND Football, start, games, coaches, players
Cross Country With the Parents A great trip from East Coast to West with the kids
Seniors, Social Security & the Minimum Wage. Things seniors need to know.
How to Write Your First Book and Publish It with CreateSpace
The US Immigration Fix--It's all in here. Finally, an answer.
I had a Dream IBM Could be #1 Again The title is self-explanatory
WineDiets.Com Presents The Wine Diet Learn how to lose weight while having fun.
Wilkes-Barre, PA; Return to Glory Wilkes-Barre City's return to glory
Geoffrey Parsons' Epoch... The Land of Fair Play Better than the original.
The Bill of Rights 4 Dummmies! This is the best book to learn about your rights.
Sol Bloom's Epoch ...Story of the Constitution The best book to learn the Constitution
America 4 Dummmies! All Americans should read to learn about this great country.
The Electoral College 4 Dummmies! How does it really work?
The All-Everything Machine Story about IBM's finest computer server.

Others can be found at amazon.com/author/brianwkelly